MAKE
ABSINTHE
GREAT AGAIN

AND OTHER COCKTAILS TO HELP
YOU SURVIVE THE TRUMP ERA

MAKE ABSINTHE GREAT AGAIN

AND OTHER COCKTAILS TO HELP YOU SURVIVE THE TRUMP ERA

by Juliet Leftwich

Photographs *by* Marshall Gordon

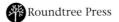

Roundtree Press

Library of Congress Cataloging-in-Publication Data available.

ISBN: 978-1-949480-03-0

10 9 8 7 6 5 4 3 2 1

Manufactured in China

Written by Juliet Leftwich
Produced and edited by Dean Burrell
Design by Maureen Forys, Happenstance Type-O-Rama
Photographs by Marshall Gordon
Technical wizardry by Dan Mitchell

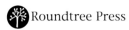Roundtree Press
149 Kentucky Street, Suite 7; Petaluma, CA 94952
707-769-1617 • www.roundtreepress.com

For Dan—my partner in crime and the best whiskey sour maker I know.

CONTENTS

WHISKEY

GIN

RUM

INTRODUCTION

ONE LAZY SUNDAY SPRING AFTERNOON, my husband, Dan, and I were having lunch and drinks at a bar in Oakland. After I asked the bartender to make a drink I had just concocted (a combination of iced coffee, Kahlúa, and other ingredients that sounded good together), Dan turned to me and casually said that I should write a book about cocktails. I'm sure he had no idea that I would immediately seize upon the idea. But it made perfect sense. I love handcrafted drinks with layered flavors and strange names, and have always enjoyed creating my own recipes. Besides, writing a book about cocktails would provide a welcome distraction from the daily news, which was driving me and everyone else I knew crazy.

Writing this book gave me an excuse to momentarily stop thinking about That Person in the White House (I will never use the words "president" and "Trump" in the same breath, since they just don't go together—kind of like the words "cat food" and "milkshake"). It also created opportunities to hang out with friends and family, experiment with combining different ingredients into interesting concoctions, and come up with a great playlist to accompany the drinks (my daughter's excellent idea). Plus, it provided a vehicle to spread the word about one of my favorite spirits—absinthe.

After much trial and error, the cocktail recipes in this book passed the taste tests of me and my crew. You should feel free, however, to experiment and tweak the recipes to suit your own palate. The idea is to try something new and have fun, and if you're really inspired, to get out on the dance floor (also sometimes known in our house as the kitchen). Take a break from the insanity and just go for it. We can all get back to worrying about how to save the world tomorrow.

TOOLS OF THE TRADE

YOU DON'T NEED A LOT of fancy equipment to make great cocktails, but it helps to have these basics:

- COCKTAIL SHAKER.

- DOUBLE-SIDED COCKTAIL JIGGER.
  Handy tip: The best jiggers hold one ounce on one side and two ounces on the other, with incremental measurements on the inside of each so you can easily see how much you're pouring.

- MIXING GLASS, strainer, and long cocktail spoon.

- CITRUS SQUEEZER. Handy tip: The best citrus squeezers have a pour spout and a flat base, so you can use them on the countertop and collect the juice in the bottom, leaving the pulp and pits in the strainer.

- WOODEN MUDDLER.

- COCKTAIL STICKS or toothpicks.

A NOTE ABOUT SIMPLE SYRUPS

MANY COCKTAILS CALL for simple syrup as a sweetener. Although you can buy simple syrup, it's really easy to make your own. Just heat equal amounts of water and sugar (say, one cup of each) in a saucepan and stir until the sugar is dissolved.

Also easy, and more fun, is to make your own flavored syrups. Popular ingredients include fresh herbs such as rosemary, mint, and basil. Here's the basic recipe:

- 1 cup water

- ¾ cup sugar (less sugar allows the herb flavor to pop)

- A handful of your herb of choice

Heat the sugar and water in a small saucepan, stirring until the sugar dissolves. Bring to a boil and add the herb. Simmer for one minute, let steep for 30 minutes and then strain. Voila—you've created your own simple syrup! The mixture will last in the fridge for about a week.

TEQUILA

Mi Casa Es Tu Casa

Resistus Interruptus

Mexican Mojito Latte

Make Absinthe Great Again (MAGA)

Zihua Dan

Mezcal Mule

TEQUILA

"Exercise makes you look better naked.
So does tequila. Your choice."

—Unknown

Some of us may be inclined to steer away from tequila because it brings back memories of the cheap tequila we consumed during our college days. But keep an open mind. Tequila has come a long way (and presumably so have you). Here are **FIVE FUN FACTS** you may not know about the spirit:

1. Tequila has its roots in a fermented drink called pulque, made by the Aztecs from the agave plant. Modern tequila was first commercially distilled in Mexico in the 1700s and 1800s, and made its American debut at the 1893 Chicago World's Fair.

2. Tequila's popularity was boosted during Prohibition, when it was smuggled into border states, and in 1968 it received international exposure during the Olympic Games in Mexico City.

3. Liquor may only be labeled "tequila" if it is produced in Mexico, primarily in the state of Jalisco, which is located in the area around the town of Tequila. It also must contain at least 51 percent of the blue agave plant.

4. The best tequilas—and really the only ones worth drinking—are made from 100 percent blue agave. Gold

tequilas contain the least amount of agave and are the least expensive (and are most likely responsible for those bad memories).

5. Clear tequilas, called "blanco" or "silver," work best in mixed drinks. Reposados (aged at least 60 days) and añejos (aged from one to three years) are the smoothest and most expensive, the latter often reserved for sipping.

Sales of high-end, premium tequilas have skyrocketed worldwide in recent years, due in part to celebrities who have jumped into the industry, and the spirit has gained a new following. So those of you who have been tequila averse, or who only drink tequila in the occasional margarita, should expand your horizons and give it another chance. You'll be pleasantly surprised.

MI CASA ES TU CASA

Why go out, when you can hang with your friends at home, mix up a batch of tasty cocktails, and crank up your favorite tunes? Welcome your guests with a refreshing Mi Casa Es Tu Casa—a contemporary version of a Tequila Sunrise—and let the fiesta begin.

- Lime wedge

- 2 tablespoons sugar for the glass rim

- 2 ounces tequila

- 6 ounces fresh orange juice

- 1 ounce fresh lime juice

- 1 ounce pomegranate juice

- 1–3 squeezes Sriracha or other hot sauce (depending on your fondness for heat)

- Lime wheel for garnish

Moisten the rim of a tall glass with a lime wedge and dip into a small plate of the sugar. Fill the glass with ice, add the remaining ingredients, and stir well. Garnish with a lime wheel.

Playlist selection: "My House," Flo Rida

RESISTUS INTERRUPTUS

A nation divided—it's us against them. Who's right? We are, of course, but being right all the time is exhausting! Take a break from the battle with a soothing Resistus Interruptus and just enjoy the magic of the party. The crazy train will come to a stop eventually.

- ₩ **1½ ounces tequila**

- ₩ **4 ounces pineapple juice**

- ₩ **½ ounce fresh lime juice**

- ₩ **1½ ounces unsweetened coconut milk**

- ₩ **Pineapple wedge for garnish**

Combine all ingredients in a cocktail shaker with ice. Shake well, strain, and garnish with a wedge of pineapple. Add a pesticide-free orchid if you're feeling particularly fancy.

Playlist selection: "24K Magic," Bruno Mars

MEXICAN MOJITO LATTE

This concoction is just right for those of us who spend half of our time wondering if it's too late to have coffee and the other half wondering if it's too early to drink alcohol. Try a Mexican Mojito Latte midday and split the difference.

- ℣ ½ ounce tequila

- ℣ ¼ ounce Kahlúa

- ℣ ½ ounce mint syrup (see p. 15)

- ℣ 2 ounces coffee

- ℣ 1½ ounces half and half

- ℣ Mint sprig for garnish

Combine all ingredients in a glass with ice and stir. Garnish with a sprig of mint.

◉ Playlist selection: "In These Shoes," Bette Midler

MAKE ABSINTHE GREAT AGAIN (MAGA)

This ridiculous rallying cry makes no sense, of course, since absinthe (like America) was always great and always will be. Banned in the U.S. until 2007 because of its allegedly hallucinogenic properties, this unfairly maligned licorice-flavored elixir is an excellent addition to a surprising number of cocktails. Here, see how it transforms a traditional margarita into one with subtle yet undeniable pizzazz.

- ₩ **2 ounces tequila**
- ₩ **1½ ounces lime juice**
- ₩ **¾ ounce agave or simple syrup (see p. 15)**
- ₩ **½ ounce absinthe**
- ₩ **Lime wheel for garnish**

Combine all ingredients in a cocktail shaker with ice. Shake well. Serve straight up or over ice and garnish with a lime wheel.

⊙ **Playlist selection: "Danza Kuduro," Don Omar and Lucenzo**

ZIHUA DAN

Although best imbibed while watching the sunset in Zihuatanejo, Mexico, after a day of fishing, this tart, no-nonsense drink
can be enjoyed anywhere.

- 2 ounces tequila
- 2 ounces fresh lime juice
- 2 ounces club soda
- Lime wedge for garnish

*Combine all ingredients in a glass with ice and stir. Garnish with a wedge
of lime.*

Playlist selection: "Corazón," Maluma (featuring
Nego do Borel)

MEZCAL MULE

Give a Moscow Mule new international flair by combining tequila with a hint of its smoky cousin, mezcal, and St. Germain, a fragrant French liqueur made from elderflowers handpicked in the Swiss Alps (really, that's how they make it). The complex flavors of this cocktail will make your taste buds dance and, if all goes well, inspire the rest of you to join in!

- 1 ounce tequila
- ⅓ ounce mezcal
- 1 ounce St. Germain liqueur
- 1½ ounces fresh lime juice
- 6–8 ounces ginger beer (depending on the glass size)
- Lime wheel for garnish

Combine all ingredients in a glass with ice and stir. Garnish with a lime wheel.

Playlist selection: "Bailando," Enrique Iglesias (featuring Sean Paul)

VODKA

From Russia with Love

A.I.

Fifty Shades of Grey Goose

Putini

The Dude Abides

Ay Carumba!

VODKA

"Vodka may not be the answer,
but it's worth a shot."

—UNKNOWN

It's no surprise that vodka is the most popular spirit in America and worldwide. Its smooth, neutral flavor makes it ideal for combining with a wide variety of mixers or for drinking by itself. Plus, it's super affordable. Here are FIVE FUN FACTS you may not know about the spirit:

1. Vodka is typically made from grains like wheat, corn, or rye, but can be made from anything that can be fermented and distilled, including potatoes, honey, grapes, or even milk.

2. Vodka's country of origin is a matter of dispute, with both Russia and Poland claiming credit as its birthplace. The spirit was introduced in America after World War II and became an immediate hit. Vodka gained a reputation as being suave and stylish in the 1950s and 1960s, thanks in part to James Bond's fondness for "shaken, not stirred" martinis, and the spirit still reigns supreme.

3. Although clever marketing campaigns have led people to believe they need to spend a lot of money to drink quality vodka, that's just not the case. A 2005 *New York Times* blind taste test of twenty-one vodkas found that a thirteen dollar bottle of Smirnoff beat out all of the

high-end brands, including Grey Goose, Ketel One, Skyy, and Hangar 1.

4. Vodka has medicinal properties and apparently is effective at treating poison ivy and soothing jellyfish stings (so be sure to have some with you the next time you venture out into the woods or go to the beach).

5. Flavored vodkas have become popular in recent years, but vodka that tastes like peanut butter and jelly, whipped cream, or pumpkin pie? No thanks.

Try out the recipes here and see for yourself why vodka is the versatile superstar of the spirit world.

FROM RUSSIA WITH LOVE

Here's to the bromance between the small-handed, stable genius in the White House and his KGB pal in the Kremlin. Why would/wouldn't they be in love?

- ♖ 1¾ ounces Russian vodka
- ♖ 2½ ounces fresh orange juice (okay, in this drink you can use Tang instead, if you really want to be authentically inauthentic)
- ♖ ½ ounce fresh lime juice
- ♖ Orange curl for garnish

Combine all ingredients in a cocktail mixing glass with ice and stir well. Strain and serve straight up. Garnish with an orange curl.

🎵 **Playlist selection: "Secret Agent Man," Johnny Rivers**

A.I.

Don't despair just because robots are taking over the world. Who knows, maybe they'll have A.I. (Absinthe Intelligence) and make great bartenders. Ponder the possibilities while sipping on this delicious version of a Lemon Drop. You'll find it hard to resist.

- Ⱳ **Lemon wedge**
- Ⱳ **2 tablespoons sugar for the glass rim**
- Ⱳ **2 ounces vodka**
- Ⱳ **1½ ounces fresh Meyer lemon juice**
- Ⱳ **1 ounce simple syrup (see p. 15)**
- Ⱳ **¼ ounce absinthe**
- Ⱳ **Lemon wheel for garnish**

Moisten the rim of a glass with a lemon wedge and dip into a small plate of the sugar. Combine remaining ingredients in a cocktail shaker with ice and shake well. Serve straight up or over ice, and garnish with a lemon wheel.

◉ **Playlist selection: "Simply Irresistible," Robert Palmer**

FIFTY SHADES OF GREY GOOSE

In the mood to get in the mood? No promises, but you know what they say about oysters …

- ♆ 1 small shucked oyster
- ♆ 1 ounce Grey Goose vodka
- ♆ ¼ ounce fresh Meyer lemon juice
- ♆ 1½ tablespoons cocktail sauce
- ♆ Dab of horseradish
- ♆ 2 dashes Worcestershire sauce
- ♆ 2–3 dashes Tabasco or other hot sauce

Place the oyster in a tall shot glass. Combine the other ingredients in a cocktail shaker with ice. Shake and strain into the glass over the oyster. Down the hatch! Repeat as necessary.

Playlist selection: "That's the Way Love Goes," Janet Jackson

PUTINI

Best consumed while riding shirtless on horseback, this cocktail clearly will not put hair on your chest.

- W 2½ ounces Russian vodka
- W ¼ ounce dry vermouth
- W Olives for garnish

Combine all ingredients in a mixing glass with ice and stir well. (Sorry, Mr. Bond. Martinis are really better stirred, not shaken.) Strain and serve straight up with an olive or two.

◉ **Playlist selection: "You're So Cold," Mariah Carey**

THE DUDE ABIDES

No need for dessert when you can drink one of these sweet, creamy cocktails. Better than ice cream! The Dude would approve.

- ♕ **1 ounce vodka**
- ♕ **½ ounce Kahlúa**
- ♕ **½ ounce Disaronno Originale amaretto liqueur**
- ♕ **2 ounces half and half**

Combine all ingredients in a glass with ice and stir.

◉ **Playlist selection: "Love Shack," The B-52's**

AY CARUMBA!

Need some spice in your life? Then turn up the heat with this fiery Bloody Mary. It will do just the trick.

- ₩ Lemon wedge
- ₩ Chile-lime salt (like Tajín Clásico) for the glass rim
- ₩ 2 ounces vodka
- ₩ 1 ounce fresh Meyer lemon juice
- ₩ 5 ounces tomato or vegetable juice
- ₩ ¼ teaspoon horseradish
- ₩ 3 dashes Worcestershire sauce
- ₩ 4–5 dashes Tabasco or other hot sauce
- ₩ Celery stalk, cherry tomato, and pepperoncini pepper for garnish

Moisten the rim of a tall glass with a lemon wedge and dip into a small plate of chile-lime salt. Fill a cocktail shaker with the remaining ingredients and shake well. Strain and serve in a tall glass over ice. Garnish with a celery stalk, cherry tomato, and pepperoncini pepper.

Playlist selection: "Conga," Gloria Estefan and Miami Sound Machine

WHISKEY

Impeachment Punch

Space Force Forever

Hi Maintenance

Death by Tweet

Faster than a Speeding Bulleit

Absinthe Makes the Heart Grow Fonder

WHISKEY

*"I love water, especially frozen into cubes
and surrounded by a delicious cocktail."*
—UNKNOWN

Retro cocktails are in, and whiskey drinks are about as retro as you can get, since Americans have been distilling whiskey since colonial days. Here are FIVE FUN FACTS about this multifaceted spirit:

1. Whiskey is produced from fermented grains, including barley, corn, rye, or wheat, and aged in wooden barrels, usually of white oak.

2. Whiskey is made worldwide, but the biggest producers are in Scotland, Ireland, Canada, and the U.S. The term "Scotch" only refers to Scottish whisky (spelled without an "e"), and more Scotch is consumed per capita in Singapore than in any other country.

3. The most popular American whiskeys include bourbon, which is made primarily from corn and is slightly sweet, and Tennessee whiskey, also made from corn but filtered through sugar-maple charcoal after distillation.

4. Although the manufacture and sale of intoxicating liquor was banned during Prohibition, the law contained exceptions for sacramental wine and for liquor prescribed for "medicinal purposes." The government granted licenses to

six whiskey distilleries to bottle and sell "medicinal whiskey," allowing people to buy whiskey with a doctor's prescription (sound familiar?). During the 1920s, the number of Walgreens Pharmacy locations soared from around twenty to more than five hundred. According to Walgreens, its unprecedented profits during that time period were due to its introduction of the milkshake.

5. Because wooden barrels are porous, approximately 4 percent of all whiskey is lost to evaporation. This loss is called the "angel's tax" or "angel's share."

Now that you know everything you need to know about whiskey, go ahead and try some. If you've tended to avoid the spirit because it seems a little intense—bringing to mind visions of cowboys throwing back shots in a saloon, or Mad Men imbibing at the office—think again. Whiskey can provide an elegant backdrop for many delicious concoctions.

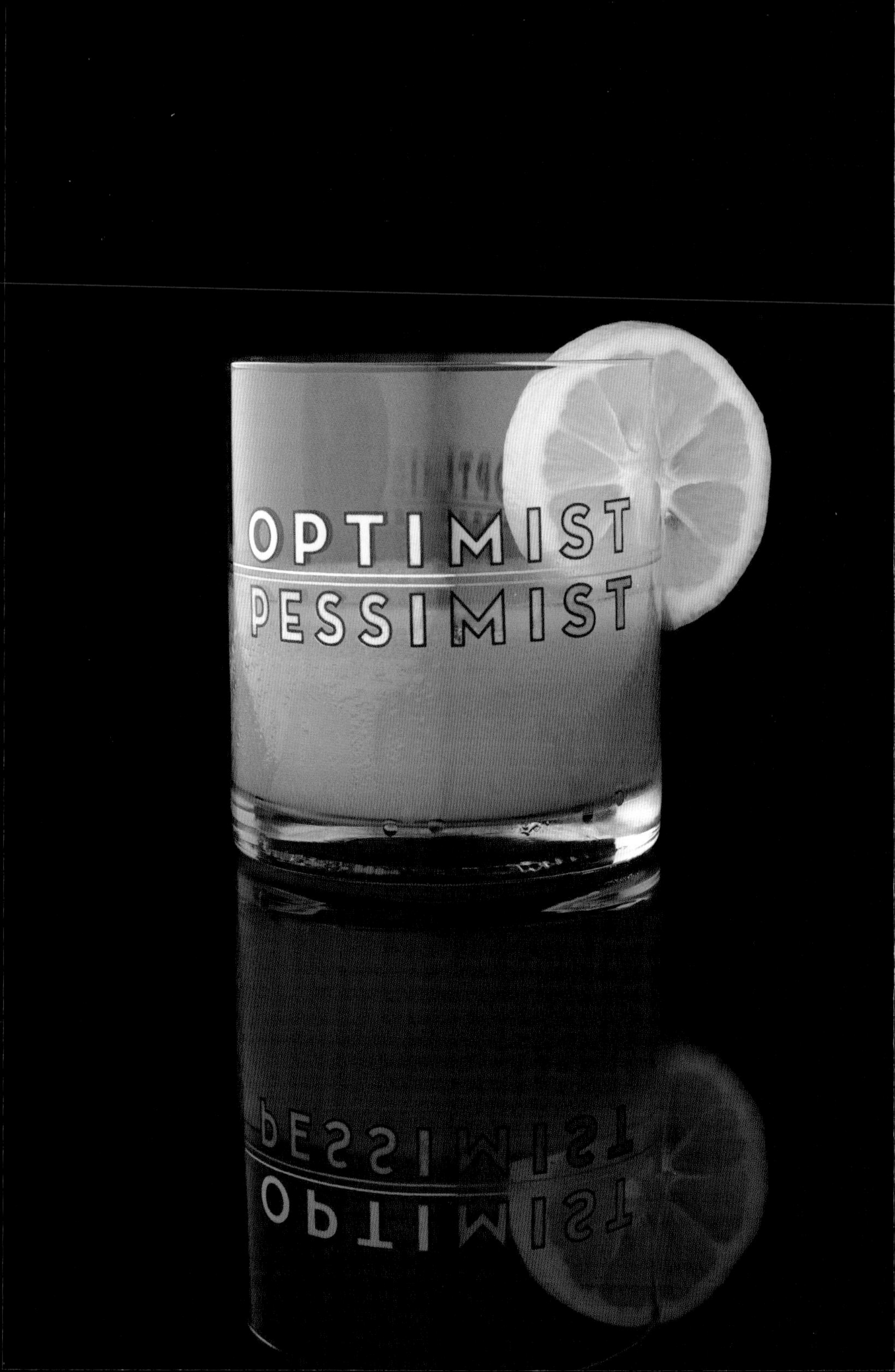
OPTIMIST
PESSIMIST

IMPEACHMENT PUNCH

High crimes and misdemeanors? Where to start? But stay optimistic—one way or another, Agent Orange is on his way out.

- ₩ **2 ounces bourbon**
- ₩ **½ ounce fresh Meyer lemon juice**
- ₩ **4 ounces peach nectar**
- ₩ **2–3 shakes curry powder**
- ₩ **Lemon wheel for garnish**

Combine all ingredients in a shaker filled with ice. Shake well and serve straight up. Garnish with a lemon wheel.

Playlist selection: "Hit the Road Jack," Ray Charles

SPACE FORCE FOREVER

Beam me up, Scottie, I need a drink. And this one's perfect for those days when you're weary from intergalactic travel with the Space Force and just want to get back to your homies. Guaranteed to help you to live long and prosper.

- ♈ **2 ounces single malt Scotch**
- ♈ **¾ ounce Drambuie**
- ♈ **½ ounce rosemary syrup (see p. 15)**
- ♈ **½ ounce fresh Meyer lemon juice**
- ♈ **Rosemary sprig for garnish**

Combine all ingredients over ice, stir, and garnish with a sprig of rosemary.

💿 **Playlist selection: "Major Tom (Coming Home)," Peter Schilling**

HI MAINTENANCE

When you order a whiskey sour, don't be shy to ask whether the bartender uses egg whites. While this inquiry may annoy your companions, it really just shows how sophisticated you are. Classic whiskey sours have always been made with egg whites. How else could one get that perfect frothy texture?

- ♕ **2 ounces bourbon**
- ♕ **1 ounce fresh Meyer lemon juice**
- ♕ **½ ounce simple syrup (see p. 15)**
- ♕ **1 egg white**
- ♕ **Fancy dark cocktail cherries (not those with Red Dye No. 2) for garnish**

Combine all ingredients in a cocktail shaker with ice. Shake vigorously, strain, and serve straight up. Garnish with a cherry or two.

◎ **Playlist selection: "My Prerogative," Bobby Brown**

DEATH BY TWEET

Can't someone please just make the torture stop? The Toddler in Chief's bizarre use OF capitalization alone Is ENOUGH To drive US all Insane! Have a warm, chocolatey Death by Tweet, and you'll feel the stress start to melt away.

- W 6–8 ounces whole milk
- W 1 serving of hot cocoa mix (the higher the cocoa content the better)
- W 1½ ounces bourbon
- W ½ ounce rum
- W Dollop of whipped cream
- W Nutmeg sprinkle
- W Mint sprig for garnish

Heat the milk, add the cocoa, and mix thoroughly. Stir in the bourbon and rum. Top with whipped cream and a sprinkle of nutmeg. Garnish with a mint sprig.

Playlist Selection: "Lips Are Movin," Meghan Trainor

FASTER THAN A
SPEEDING BULLEIT

"More powerful than a locomotive! Able to leap tall buildings in a single bound! Look! Up in the sky! It's a bird! It's a plane! It's Superman!" Actually, it's just a really strong drink.

- W **1½ ounces Bulleit bourbon**
- W **1 ounce raspberry liqueur**
- W **Rasberries for garnish**

Combine the bourbon and raspberry liqueur in a glass with ice. Stir and garnish with a raspberry or two.

Playlist selection: "Saving My Life," Gorgon City (featuring ROMANS)

ABSINTHE MAKES THE HEART GROW FONDER

Absinthe is a potent spirit made with anise and other botanicals mixed with *Artemisia absinthium* (wormwood). Traditionally served with water poured over a sugar cube on a slotted spoon, absinthe rose to great popularity in Paris among intellectuals and bohemian artists like Vincent van Gogh, Toulouse-Lautrec, and Pablo Picasso. French society was scandalized and unfairly blamed the "Green Fairy" for immoral behavior, even murder, leading to its nearly worldwide ban. But absinthe is back! Try it in this cocktail and see why Oscar Wilde once asked, "What difference is there between a glass of absinthe and a sunset?"

- ⚘ 2 ounces bourbon

- ⚘ ½ ounce absinthe

- ⚘ ¼ ounce simple syrup (see p. 15)

- ⚘ ½ ounce fresh Meyer lemon juice

- ⚘ Lemon wedge for garnish

Combine all ingredients in a shaker filled with ice. Shake well and serve over ice with a lemon wedge garnish.

◉ Playlist selection: "Say Amen (Saturday Night)," Panic! at the Disco

GIN

Notorious RBG

Covfefe Cooler

Ferris Wheel

Pura Vida

Mango Unchained

We Want You Back!

GIN

"In alcohol's defense, I've done some pretty dumb shit while completely sober, too."
—UNKNOWN

Gin is a juniper-based spirit known for having inspired more classic cocktails than any other type of liquor. As part of the cocktail renaissance, gin is quite en vogue these days, and gin-only bars are popping up around the country. Here are FIVE FUN FACTS about the spirit:

1. Although most associated with England, gin has its roots in Dutch genever, invented by a physician in the sixteenth century as a medicine. During the Dutch War of Independence, it was given to soldiers as "Dutch courage."

2. The gin and tonic—the quintessential English cocktail—dates back to nineteenth century India. British officers drank tonic water (which contained bitter quinine) to avoid malaria, adding gin to make it more palatable.

3. Prohibition was known for "bathtub gin," homemade liquor that was notorious for its bad taste and dangerous ingredients.

4. Many vodka cocktails, like martinis and gimlets, were originally made with gin. As vodka became popular in the 1950s and 1960s, however, it became common to

substitute it for gin, since vodka was cheaper and had a milder flavor.

5. Juniper berries are the main ingredient in gin, but they aren't really berries—they're more like tiny pinecones. Gin flavors vary widely depending on the other botanicals that are used, including cardamom, black pepper, lavender, and citrus.

Gin is meant for cocktails (you've never seen anyone do gin shots, right?), and its complex, nuanced flavor makes it an excellent choice for creating one-of-a-kind drinks. Try the recipes here, and if you aren't already a gin fan, you're sure to become a convert.

NOTORIOUS RBG

Raise a glass to one of the most iconic Supreme Court justices in American history. May Ruth's truths live on forever!

- ♕ 1 ounce gin
- ♕ 1 ounce fresh Meyer lemon juice
- ♕ ½ ounce simple syrup (see p. 15)
- ♕ 4 ounces Champagne
- ♕ Curled lemon peel for garnish

Combine the first three ingredients in a cocktail mixing glass with ice and stir well. Strain the ice and pour the mixture into a Champagne flute. Top with Champagne and garnish with a curled lemon peel.

◉ Playlist selection: "Respect," Aretha Franklin

COVFEFE COOLER

There are no words except "SAD!!"

- ♕ 1 ounce gin
- ♕ 1 ounce Russian vodka
- ♕ 5 ounces fresh orange juice
- ♕ ½ ounce fresh lime juice
- ♕ 1 ounce pomegranate juice
- ♕ 4 dashes orange bitters (more if you're feeling particularly bitter)

Combine all ingredients over ice, stir, and drown your/our sorrows. No garnish is necessary, but add an orchid (pesticide-free) if you like.

💿 **Playlist selection: "Toxic," Britney Spears**

FERRIS WHEEL

Bueller, Bueller, Bueller …? Go ahead, take the day off. You deserve it. And you deserve this delicious version of a Ramos Gin Fizz, the perfect brunch cocktail. Invented in 1888 by New Orleans saloon owner Henry C. Ramos, this light, frothy drink became an immediate hit. Try it and you'll see why its popularity has endured.

- ♈ **2 ounces gin**
- ♈ **½ ounce fresh lime juice**
- ♈ **½ ounce fresh Meyer lemon juice**
- ♈ **½ ounce simple syrup (see p. 15)**
- ♈ **1 egg white**
- ♈ **4–5 dashes orange blossom water**
- ♈ **Nutmeg sprinkle**
- ♈ **Lime wheel for garnish**

Combine all ingredients except the nutmeg in a cocktail shaker without ice and shake. Add ice and shake well again (you have to work a bit to get that perfect fluffy texture). Strain into a glass and top with a sprinkle of nutmeg. Garnish with a lime wheel.

🎵 **Playlist selection: "Twist and Shout," The Beatles**

PURA VIDA

"Pura Vida" is more than just an expression in Costa Rica—it's a way of life, a philosophy, if you will. Costa Ricans use the term, which means "pure life" or "simple life," to say hello or good-bye, as a toast, or just to say "no worries, don't stress." So take a sip of this refreshing cocktail and just be happy. Pura Vida, my friends!

- 1½ ounces gin
- 3 ounces pineapple juice
- 1½ ounces apricot juice
- 2 ounces unsweetened coconut milk
- ½ ounce fresh Meyer lemon juice
- Pineapple wedge for garnish

Combine all ingredients in a cocktail shaker with ice and shake. Strain and serve in a tall glass over ice. Garnish with a pineapple wedge.

Playlist selection: "Happy," Pharrell Williams

MANGO UNCHAINED

Like the main character in the movie (which some of us were too faint-hearted to watch), you, too, can be a hero. No violence need be involved, however. Just get yourself and everyone you know out to the polls to vote. Contemplate your favorite candidates while savoring a sweet and tart Mango Unchained.

- ₩ 1½ ounces gin

- ₩ 3 ounces mango nectar

- ₩ ¾ ounce fresh lime juice

- ₩ Lime wheel for garnish

Combine all ingredients in a cocktail shaker with ice and shake well. Strain and serve straight up or over ice. Garnish with a lime wheel.

🔘 **Playlist selection: "Chained to the Rhythm," Katy Perry (featuring Skip Marley)**

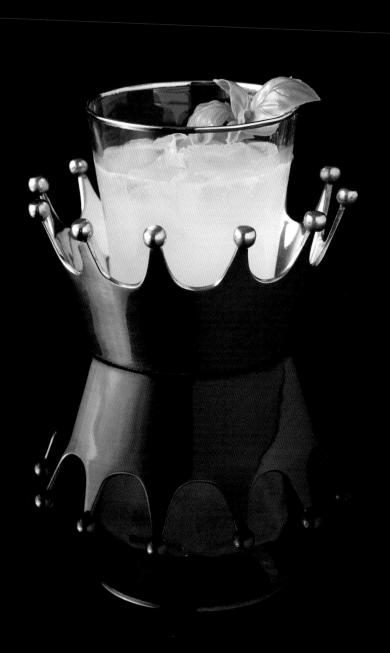

WE WANT YOU BACK!

Was it all just a dream, or was the last occupant of the White House brilliant, honorable, gracious, and so cool that he could sing "Let's Stay Together" almost as well as Al Green himself? We knew we'd miss him, but OMG!! Crying face emoji.

- ₩ Basil leaves (about 8), plus one sprig for garnish
- ₩ 2 ounces gin
- ₩ ½ ounce simple syrup (see p. 15)
- ₩ 1 ounce fresh lime juice

Place the basil leaves in your hand and clap to release the oils. Combine the basil leaves, simple syrup, and lime juice in a cocktail shaker and muddle well. Add gin and ice, and shake thoroughly. Strain and serve over ice. Garnish with a sprig of basil.

◎ Playlist selection: "Miss You," The Rolling Stones

RUM

Havana Heartbreak

Belize Kiss

Dark and Stormy Daniels

Reggae on the Rocks

Tikilicious

Carpe Diem Punch

RUM

"Rum won't solve your problems.
Then again, neither will milk."

—UNKNOWN

Looking for a spirit that can be sipped or used in an umbrella-worthy cocktail, is reasonably priced, and can be used in a delicious scorpion bowl to share with your friends? Check, check, and check. Here are FIVE FUN FACTS about rum:

1. Rum has its roots in the Caribbean and is made from sugarcane byproducts, typically molasses, or from sugarcane juice. The first rum distilleries began operating in Barbados in the early seventeenth century.

2. Rum was the preferred alcoholic drink of pirates and the British Royal Navy. British sailors were given a daily rum ration from 1655 until 1970 (1970!).

3. George Washington was a huge rum fan. He gave rum and other types of alcohol to prospective voters in 1758 when he campaigned for the Virginia House of Burgess, and had rum brought in from Barbados for his presidential inauguration.

4. Several famous rum drinks—like the mojito, Cuba Libre, and daiquiri (Ernest Hemingway's alleged favorite)— were invented in Cuba. During Prohibition, American

tourists and bartenders flooded into Havana, known for its sophisticated nightlife.

5. "Proof" is a method of measuring the alcohol content of liquor. In the U.S., proof is defined as twice the alcohol content by volume (so 80 proof rum contains 40 percent alcohol). Back in the day, sailors would mix rum with gunpowder and light it on fire to "prove" it was the real thing. If it didn't ignite, they knew it had been watered down. You learn something every day, right?

Rum comes in a variety of types and colors, but aged rums are generally the tastiest. Do your own taste test to see which ones you like the best and then try your favorite in these cocktails. Soon you'll discover why rum is the spirit that has something for everyone.

HAVANA HEARTBREAK

They met while strolling along the Malecón—she the adventurous Americana and he the handsome Cubano. They toasted to newfound romance at Floridita's and kissed under the stars, but alas, their love was not to be.

- ₩ Mint leaves (about 8), plus a sprig for garnish
- ₩ 1 ounce simple syrup (see p. 15)
- ₩ 1½ ounces fresh lime juice
- ₩ 2 ounces rum
- ₩ 2 dashes Angostura bitters
- ₩ Curled lime peel for garnish
- ₩ Teardrops optional

Place the mint leaves in your hand and clap to release the oils. Combine the mint leaves, simple syrup, and lime juice in a cocktail shaker and muddle well. Add the rum and bitters with ice, and shake thoroughly. Strain into a glass (straight up or over ice) and garnish with the mint sprig and curled lime peel.

◉ Playlist selection: "Havana," Camila Cabello (featuring Young Thug)

BELIZE KISS

Turquoise waters, great food, friendly people. What's not to love about Belize? Try this delicious tropical drink, and you'll imagine you're there. A Belize Kiss, meant for two, will put everything in perspective and bring you closer to the one you love.

- W 2½ ounces rum
- W 4 ounces pineapple juice
- W 2 ounces fresh orange juice
- W 1 ounce fresh lime juice
- W 2 ounces unsweetened coconut milk
- W Pineapple wedge for garnish

Combine all ingredients in a blender with ice and blend until frothy. Garnish with a pineapple wedge. Serves two.

Playlist selection: "Love of My Life," Santana (featuring Dave Matthews)

DARK AND
STORMY DANIELS

It's best to have this one at home. If you don't, it could end up costing you $130,000 and a spanking.

- Mint leaves (about 8), plus a sprig for garnish
- 2 ounces rum
- 1 ounce fresh lime juice
- Ginger beer (6–8 ounces depending on the glass size)

Place the mint leaves in your hand and clap to release the oils. Combine the mint leaves, rum, and lime juice in the bottom of a tall glass and muddle well. Add ice and the ginger beer. Garnish with a sprig of mint.

Playlist selection: "Payback," Rascal Flatts

REGGAE
ON THE ROCKS

The distant sound of steel drums, the cool sea breeze, the slight scent of ganja in the air. Are you in Jamaica or in Berkeley? Either way, a Reggae on the Rocks is just the thing to quench your thirst and help keep you mellow.

- ♕ **1 ounce rum**
- ♕ **1 ounce gin**
- ♕ **2 ounces fresh lime juice**
- ♕ **4–6 ounces cola**
- ♕ **3 shakes Angostura bitters**
- ♕ **Lime wheel for garnish**

Combine all ingredients over ice, stir, and garnish with a lime wheel.

◉ **Playlist selection: "Jamming," Bob Marley and The Wailers**

TIKILICIOUS

Tiki aficionados are automatically drawn to mysterious tropical establishments with exotic drinks, dark lighting, and unique decor (blowfish lights, anyone?). Have a Tikilicious, and you may just become a member of the cult.

- 2 ounces rum
- 5 ounces pomegranate juice
- 2 ounces pineapple juice
- 1 ounce unsweetened coconut milk

Combine all ingredients in a cocktail shaker with ice. Shake well, strain, and serve in a tall glass over ice.

Playlist selection: "El Tiki," Maluma

CARPE DIEM PUNCH

Seize the day. **YOLO**. Life is short. All of these expressions have the same message: be happy you're alive today. So grab some extra-long straws and share a delicious bowl of Carpe Diem Punch with people you care about. It's time to celebrate.

- 2 cups rum
- 1 cup pineapple juice
- 1 cup fresh orange juice
- 1 cup guava nectar
- 1 cup peach nectar
- 1 cup mango nectar
- ¼ cup fresh lime juice
- ¼ cup fresh Meyer lemon juice
- Gardenia (pesticide-free)

Combine all ingredients in a large bowl filled with ice and stir. Garnish with a gardenia and enjoy! Serves 6–8.

🔘 **Playlist selection: "Adventure of a Lifetime," Coldplay**

PLAYLIST

- "My House," Flo Rida
- "24K Magic," Bruno Mars
- "In These Shoes," Bette Midler
- "Danzo Kuduro," Don Omar and Lucenzo
- "Corazón," Maluma (featuring Nego do Borel)
- "Bailando," Enrique Iglesias (featuring Sean Paul)
- "Secret Agent Man," Johnny Rivers
- "Simply Irresistible," Robert Palmer
- "That's the Way Love Goes," Janet Jackson
- "You're So Cold," Mariah Carey
- "Love Shack," The B-52's
- "Conga," Gloria Estefan and Miami Sound Machine
- "Hit the Road Jack," Ray Charles
- "Major Tom (Coming Home)," Peter Schilling
- "My Prerogative," Bobby Brown
- "Lips are Movin," Meghan Trainor
- "Saving My Life," Gorgon City (featuring ROMANS)
- "Say Amen (Saturday Night)," Panic! at the Disco
- "Respect," Aretha Franklin
- "Toxic," Britney Spears
- "Twist and Shout," The Beatles
- "Happy," Pharrell Williams
- "Chained to the Rhythm," Katy Perry (featuring Skip Marley)
- "Miss You," The Rolling Stones

- "Havana," Camila Cabello (featuring Young Thug)
- "Love of My Life," Santana (featuring Dave Matthews)
- "Payback," Rascal Flatts
- "Jamming," Bob Marley and The Wailers
- "El Tiki," Maluma
- "Adventure of a Lifetime," Coldplay

BONUS TRACKS

Dance Tunes

- "Where the Party At," Jagged Edge (featuring Nelly)
- "Thong Song," Sisqó
- "Get Down Tonight," KC and The Sunshine Band
- "We've Got it Goin' On," Backstreet Boys
- "Beat It," Michael Jackson
- "Can't Feel My Face," The Weeknd

And for Something a Little Different

- "I've Seen that Face Before (Libertango)," Grace Jones
- "Lost on You," LP
- "Don't Wanna Fight," Alabama Shakes
- "Tadow," Masego and FKJ
- "California Roll," Snoop Dogg (featuring Stevie Wonder)
- "Bellyache," Billie Eilish (Marian Hill Remix)

ACKNOWLEDGMENTS

MANY THANKS TO MY HUSBAND, Dan Rapaport, for providing the inspiration for this book and for being an excellent sounding board and taste tester throughout the process. I'm also very grateful to our kids, Jake and Gina Rapaport, and to Jake's wife, Talia, and Gina's fiancé, Scott Bogdanoff, for their invaluable encouragement and support. Special thanks to Gina who, knowing my passion for music and obsession with playlists, suggested that I pair each drink with a song.

I greatly appreciate the professional assistance I received during this project. Thanks to Pamela Livingston for enthusiastically embracing the concept of the book and for introducing me to my editor and advisor, Dean Burrell. Dean educated me about the publishing world, giving me excellent advice each step of the way, and brought designer extraordinaire Maureen Forys onto the team. I'm also very grateful to my photographer, Marshall Gordon, and his colleague, Technical Wizard Dan Mitchell, for making my vision of the photos a reality. I enjoyed playing set designer during the photo shoots and was incredibly impressed by their artistry and attention to detail (who knew it could be so difficult to make a mint sprig garnish look perfect?).

I'm also very thankful for the help of our many family friends, including Donn and Jan Pickett, who spent much of a long weekend in Zihuatanejo brainstorming about drink names (I still like Margarita Schmargarita, but was outvoted) and several Sunday afternoons sampling recipes. A shout out, too, to my former colleagues at the Giffords Law Center to Prevent Gun Violence who, in addition to working tirelessly to combat gun violence nationwide, really know how to have a good time. Viva Tequila Thursday! Particular thanks to Ari Freilich for giving me permission to steal the name of the drink he invented, Mango Unchained.

I also want to acknowledge my longtime friends Ann Gibbons, whom I've known since age thirteen, and Tracey Borst, my college roommate. We had a lot of good times and bad cocktails when we were young, and I'm so glad we're still close.

Finally, I want to thank my sisters, Sue, Janet, Francy, and Margie, for a lifetime of joy and laughter; and our wonderful mom, Ellen Leftwich, the OG, for teaching us that love conquers all and that one should never underestimate the value of a good party (or a good drink).

A toast to all the people throughout my life who have given me roots so that I could grow wings and fly. Salud!

INDEX

ABOUT THE AUTHOR

JULIET LEFTWICH is an attorney and a social justice advocate who lives in Berkeley, California, with her husband and favorite mixologist, Dan Rapaport.